Chemical Engineers WHERE Do We Work?

Diana Tran

To my brother for being my editor.

To fellow colleagues that represent the

chemical engineering community.

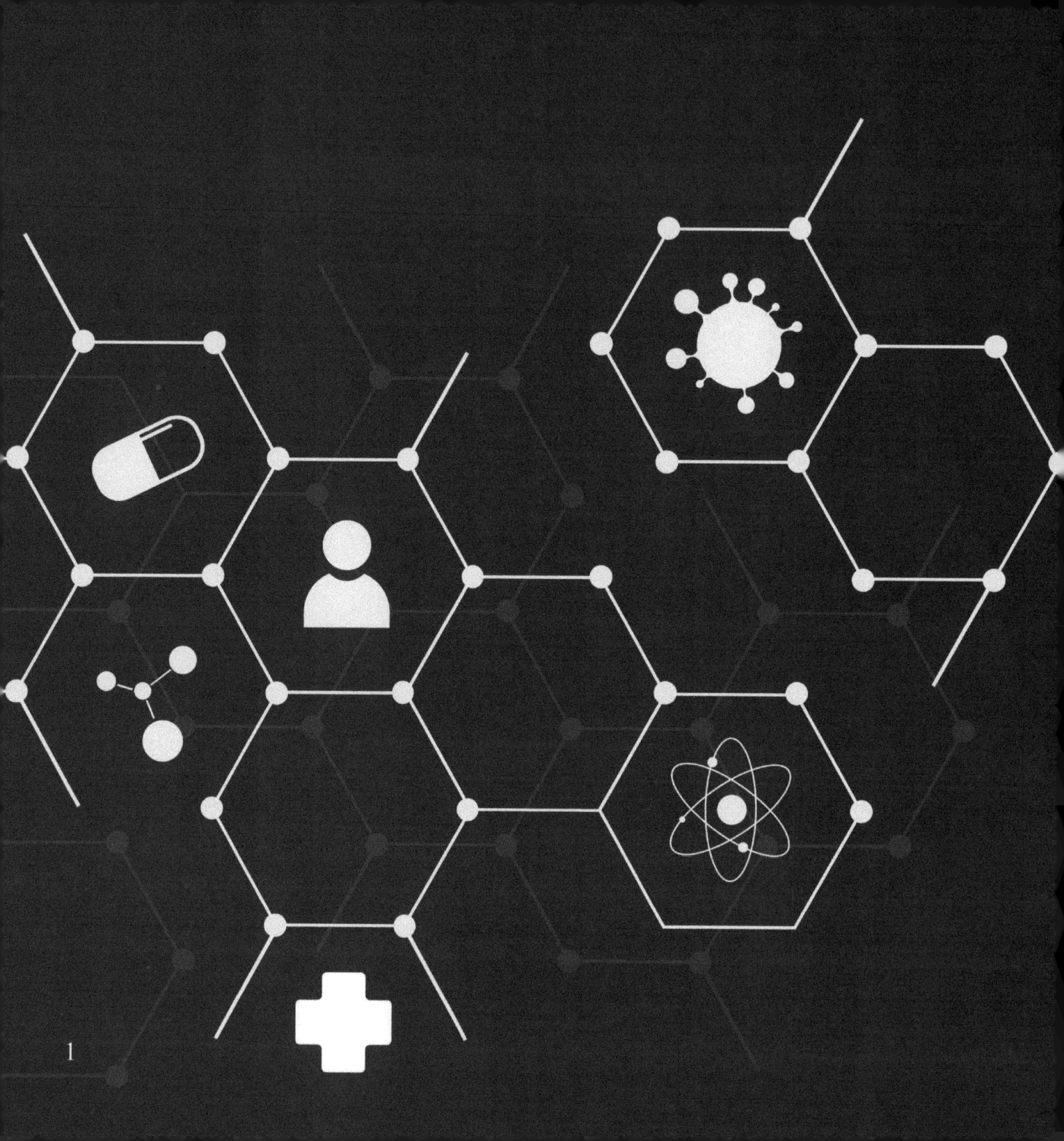

Dear Readers,

    Hello. You have picked up this book and have reached this page, which is great. Please continue. If it was purely out of curiosity that you stumbled upon this book, I hope this sparks your interest to know more about chemical engineers and where we work in the world.

    Happy reading from **A** to **Z** !

My name is **A**nna. I work at the University as a lecturer teaching the fundamentals of chemical engineering to the next generation.

My name is **B**arry. I work at a glass processing plant that makes glass bottles for the beverage industry.

My name is **C**laire. I work at a potato chip factory that uses new technologies to improve the taste and nutrition of your snacks.

My name is **D**aniel. I work at a water treatment plant in operations to ensure that the community receives clean water to drink.

My name is **E**mily. I work in a laboratory that tests the quality of skin care products to ensure their properties are correct.

My name is **F**red. I work at a mining site that extracts and produces important metals and minerals.

My name is **G**eorgia. I work at a beer production plant crafting different beer varieties by changing the process operating conditions.

Note. Legal drinking age – 18 or older.

My name is **H**uynh. I work in a wastewater treatment plant treating sewage waste to produce recycled water for agricultural usage.

My name is **I**sabelle. I work in a vineyard to produce the best grapes for wine production.

My name is **J**ohn. I work in the pharmaceutical industry creating and managing specialty medical supplies.

My name is **K**ylie. I work with rural communities in developing regions to produce safe quality drinking water.

My name is **L**iam. I work in an engineering consulting company providing cost-effective solutions to projects for clients.

My name is **M**ary. I am the founder and chief executive officer (CEO) of my own business bringing innovative ideas to life.

My name is **N**athan. I design and supervise the construction of manufacturing plants for clients.

My name is **O**lga. I work in health services to create and enhance pharmaceutical formulations and drug delivery systems.

My name is **P**aul. I work in a biomanufacturing facility that develops and produces covid vaccines.

My name is **Q**uinn. I work at a chocolate manufacturing facility ensuring you receive great texture and taste in every chocolate bite.

My name is **R**yan. I work in financial analytics and data processing to find ways to optimise an organisation's operations.

My name is **S**tefanie. I work in a high-tech greenhouse facility that uses renewable sources to grow fruits and vegetables.

H$_2$
HYDROGEN

NH$_3$
AMMONIA

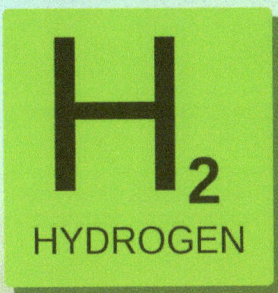

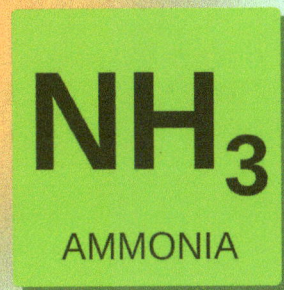

My name is **T**imothy. I work for a start-up company focused on producing green energy for the future.

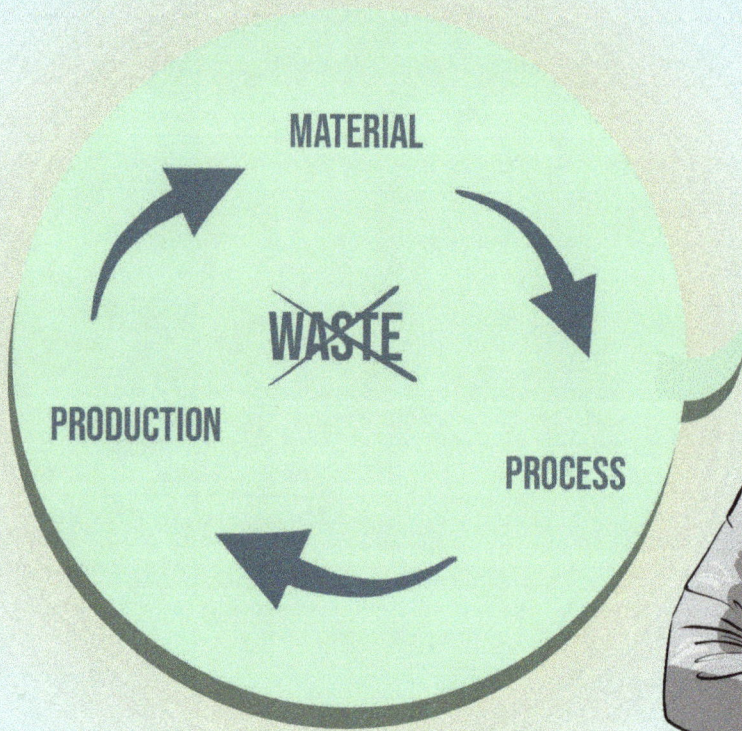

My name is **U**ma. I am a university professor focused on developing sustainable techniques in processing systems to minimise waste.

My name is **V**incent. I work in a recycling facility finding innovative ways to reuse plastic waste.

My name is **W**endy. I work in the gas industry using software to anticipate equipment failure along the pipeline that can impact supply and process safety.

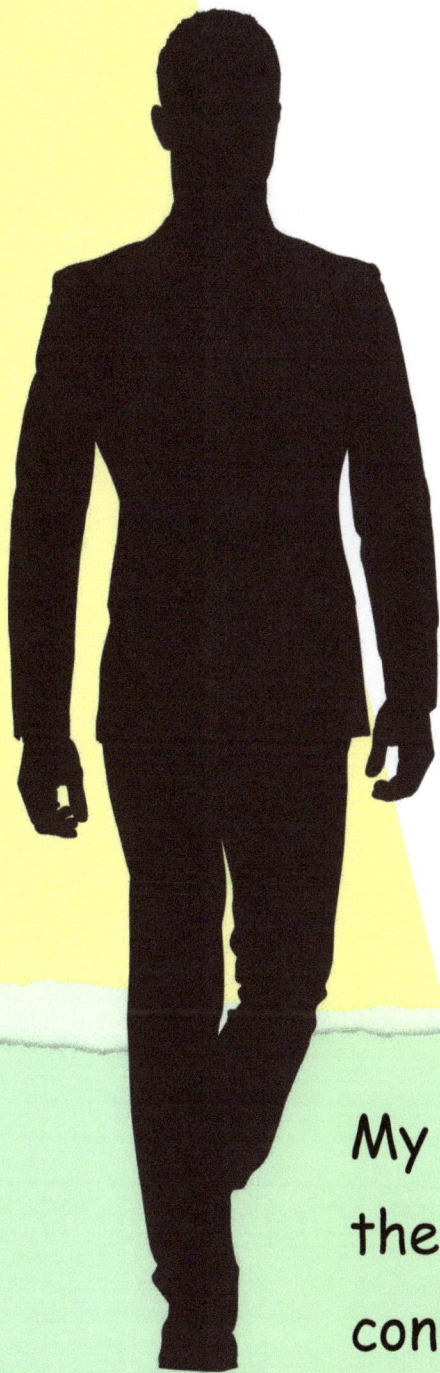

CONFIDENTIAL

My name is **X**avier. I work in the defence sector, which is confidential so I cannot tell you.

My name is **Y**asmin. I work in a cosmetic manufacturing facility that specialises in the formulation of beauty products.

My name is **Z**ac. I work in the government sector ensuring processing and manufacturing plants comply with regulations, legislation, and policy guidelines.

Let's work together!

The End

Also by Diana Tran

Chemical Engineering
Made Simple

Process
to
Progress

Diana Tran

www.ingramcontent.com/pod-product-compliance
Lightning Source LLC
Chambersburg PA
CBHW040250100426
42811CB00011B/1209